T0146784

SHAPING THE LIVES OF OUR CHILDREN

Parenting is not a friendship

LES RODGERS

authorHOUSE®

AuthorHouse™
1663 Liberty Drive
Bloomington, IN 47403
www.authorhouse.com
Phone: 1 (800) 839-8640

Published by AuthorHouse 02/23/2016

ISBN: 978-1-5049-7914-6 (sc)
ISBN: 978-1-5049-7912-2 (hc)
ISBN: 978-1-5049-7913-9 (e)

Library of Congress Control Number: 2016902229

Print information available on the last page.

Table of Contents

Dedication-

To every parent and person supporting, encouraging, and caring for our children; this book is dedicated to you. For all of your sacrifices past and to come, I thank you for never giving up on our children. I am sure that because of you, many children will grow to become confident and productive role models to others, and eventually, together, we will change the world. Our children are that glimmer of hope for a changed tomorrow, so kudos to you for all you do!

I also dedicate this book to my mother for all the sacrifices she has made for me and my six brothers and sisters. Her courage and support allowed me to dream and believe that the life I wanted was possible. Thanks Mom, I love you and owe every accomplishment to you.

To my two daughters, I thank you for being open to my advice, guidance, and tough love. You are the example that parents can make a difference.

Lastly, but definitely not least; I dedicate this book to my wife Ya Sonda "Monique." You have been such an inspiration, and this book would not have materialized without your encouragement. I thank you for believing in me and for being my greatest cheerleader.

-Introduction-

A parent's involvement in a child's life has proven to be essential in developing a well-rounded, respectful, and driven individual. Parental involvement is comprised of several key components ; including the parents' belief that their involvement is important in their children's development, and has expectations of their children's success; but more importantly the way in which a parent becomes involved is essential. The "Shaping the Lives of Our Children" concept identifies those key components and provides clear direction for parents and their children. The earlier parents become involved, the more powerful the effect.

Children ages 3-5 are like sponges because:

- ♥ They begin to understand the feelings of others and are developing control of their own feelings.

- ♥ They are capable of taking turns and following instructions.

- ♥ They are capable of learning right from wrong.

- ♥ They are capable of learning boundaries.

- ♥ Parents can establish parental authority.

- ♥ They are open to expressions of love, affection, and play.

That tantrum throwing, screaming child wailing and kicking on the floor at Walmart, does not necessarily need medication and the answer is not to purchase the toy he or she is campaigning for. Whether you are the, "take a time out" disciplinarian, or believe Proverbs: 29:15 KJV, "The rod of correction imparts wisdom, but a child left by itself disgraces it's mother," something needs to have occurred at home to prevent that Walmart display of no, or minimal home training.

"Train up a child in the way he should go and when he is old, he will not depart from it (Proverbs 22:6, KJV). Translation: whatever a child does at home will spread abroad because proper training begins and is reinforced in the home. Home is the training ground for life. It is not a teacher's responsibility to rear our children.

Although teachers are greatly influential and spend more hours during the week with our children, the seed for proper growth is planted at home. We must send our children to school prepared to learn. Parents have such a great impact that even the success of our school systems depend largely on support from parents. If we are to improve our schools, we must become more involved in the schools our children attend. Most of us have little time to volunteer, but some participation by all parents would make the difference.

We can continue to make a difference from their childhood through early adulthood.

Our preteen, teen, and children in early adulthood are presented with challenges that can be far more devastating than challenges they face in the earlier years. Those challenges can sometimes be irreversible. We release our children into a world plagued by:

- ✓ Gangs - Fear that they will join and/or become victim to gang activity

- ✓ Violence / Crime – Fear they will be in the wrong place at the wrong time, or choose the wrong friends

- ✓ Drugs – Become a drug user or drug trafficker

- ✓ Cyber Crime - Internet safety concerns (Human trafficking, bullying, "Stranger Danger")

✓ Teen pregnancy and sexually transmitted diseases- Being influenced by the media and their peers to engage in premarital and promiscuous sex

✓ Peer pressure – Making bad decisions as they try to fit in

Our preteens, teens, and young adults are also faced with:

✓ Discipline - Staying focused and avoiding those things that cause disruptions in their lives

✓ Respecting authority – Teachers, law enforcement, rules and regulations

✓ Self-respect – Knowing what it really means to love oneself

✓ Dreams and purpose – What do I want to do with my life, and how am I going to do it?

So whether you are expecting children, have young children, preteens, teens, or young adults, your loved ones can have the life they deserve; but it will require your help. That help begins with your state of mind. Digest the following as food for thought.

Decades of research show that when parents are involved, children have:

♥ Higher grades, test scores and graduation rates

♥ Better school attendance

♥ Better student achievement (Academics / Sports)

♥ Higher levels of motivation and self-esteem

♥ Decreased discipline problems

♥ Lower probability of drug or alcohol use

♥ A better chance of staying out of the Criminal Justice System

CHAPTER ONE

Until now...most of us learned to parent
"The hard way"

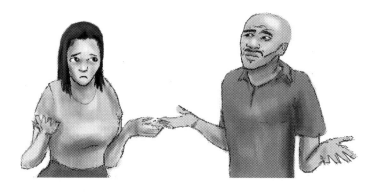

Effective parental involvement begins with the parent's state of mind. Although two parents in the household is desirable, one parent doing the right thing trumps two parents in the household where one parent is dysfunctional, counterproductive, and promoting unhealthy development in the children. Needless to say, there must be at least one parent who is parenting and not treating the child they are charged with raising like a friend. Parenting and friendship are distinctly two very different things. Unfortunately, sometimes we don't know that we are creating a friendship with the children that are depending on us for guidance, values, morals, motivation, and discipline. Yes, our children want discipline. They want to feel order, responsibility, and protection. A friendship does not offer those things. How do you know that you may be befriending your children instead of parenting? I'm glad you asked.

First and foremost, children must view their parents as figures of authority. Children should understand that the relationship with their parents is not an evenly matched relationship. Although we should allow our children to have opinions, express those opinions, and in some cases make decisions for themselves; our children must know that we are leading and that they will follow.

To the contrary, in a parent to child relationship that functions like a friendship, the relationship is viewed by the children as evenly matched in which case the parents are not viewed as authority figures. The children then become accustomed to not taking direction from their parents and begin to make their own decisions based on what they see and hear around them. This is not a desirable relationship because of the overwhelming violence, distorted images of sexual intimacy, and other negative behaviors around us that plague our world.

THIS IS NOT A NEGOTIATION

Are you telling your children what you expect of them, or are you asking their permission when it comes to decisions you should be making for them? Let me help you by sharing a story with you.

The errors of my ways cost me a great deal: sadness, anger, contributed to a failed marriage, challenged new relationships, and affected my ability to be the head of my own household. If I had only understood the hierarchy of love as designed by God,

I would have known that a child's "place" does not supersede the responsibility to a spouse and creating harmony in one's household. I learned many things about parenting when my daughters became of an age to fully display the harvest produced from every seed I had planted. I would soon learn that children are truly sponges absorbing and holding information like a sponge sitting in water. Every experience contributed to their success, as well as the parental struggles I would endure later. We create the relationships that exist with our children. The good news is that we can make adjustments to change the "friend to friend " relationship to the more desirable "parent to child" relationship. However; it is important to know that the younger the child is, the easier it is to make the adjustments that will develop the relationship with your child, pre-teen, or young adult the way God intended. "Train up a child in the way he should go, and when he is older he will not depart from it" (Proverbs 22:6, NIV). Our responsibility is to raise our children. Friendship is the benefit we enjoy when they become productive adults. So, as you might gather at this point, the message here is that we must understand that we have a responsibility to our children that can only be accomplished by parenting. When we are parenting, it's kind of like governing. The type of government that you operate within will produce different results. When it comes to raising a child, you should not be operating within a Democracy, whereas decisions would be made based on a vote between the parents and their children. We should be operating within a Dictatorship, whereas the parents' decisions do not necessarily require the children's approval or input. So maybe now is a good point to tell you something I learned about effective parenting from a particular experience I had with my children.

"Keep your feet on the floor and let go of her hair"

I have been praised for being a great father and raising two great daughters. They are young ladies who've become well-rounded, motivated, focused, driven, and all in "My business!"

Well, let me define "My business." My business is considered to be any information, concerns, comments, or opinions where I would not want my children's input or opinions, (i.e. my adult relationships or finances).

A parent's business is not child's play. It is for our eyes only, and many times our first mistake is making "IT" available to their ears. When we don't, we then find ourselves reciting those famous words, "Stay out of my business, stay out of grown folks conversation, or Am I talking to you?" In other words, we provide our children with information that they should not be concerned with by discussing matters in their presence. As they process the information, they begin to develop an opinion. We are now well on our way to having to discuss "adult business" with a child; and may have created a blurred line that should be a well-defined line. Remember, opinions can lead to feelings of entitlement causing children to ask challenging questions. When our children feel free to challenge our authority, our ability to effectively parent is compromised.

Allow me break it down further. It starts with inviting a child's advice about a decision you are contemplating. What do you want for dinner? Are you going to church with me today? We then begin to negotiate with a child to do something we should just tell them to do. "If you go to church today, you can go out and play later," when we actually should have said, "Get ready for church and when you get home and finish your chores you can go outside and play." The important thing to know is that parenting is not a friendship. When we understand and digest this, we can begin to cultivate a healthy parent to child relationship.

I married at a young age and my wife, at the time, was my exact opposite when it came to childrearing. We were young adults with a child and doing the best with what we knew at the time. I was the disciplinarian and she would soon become the voice of opposition for decisions I made. I was like any other father with two beautiful daughters; I was very protective of them. My daughters and I were very close and they were the number one priority in my life. We had an open line of communication and talked about EVERYTHING. I don't know how it began, but somehow we thought our conversations were more interesting when the three of us would cut the lights off, sit in a circle on the floor, light a candle, and then talk about anything that was on our minds. This was a time I discovered some of the things that were of concern to them. I guess it was my way of giving them my undivided attention, getting to know them, and having a couple of laughs. If you haven't realized it by now, I have not discussed how much time I spent with my wife. There's a really good reason for that. It's simple. I didn't make her much of a priority. This, my friends, created a crack in the foundation on which a healthy balanced household is built. In other words, my children did not see my wife and I as a "United Front" because we weren't. I discovered that this was true when my wife didn't support parental decisions I made regarding our daughters, and I didn't agree on decisions she made regarding our daughters. Often, when we as parents can't make up our minds, our children will begin to make decisions for, or without us. Let's look at it from a child's point of view.

"Daddy said that we can't go to that party because there's been a lot of drug use and shootings in that area."

"Well, Mommy said that daddy is overprotective because of his job and what he has seen."

So, as you might have guessed, my daughters asked me again if they could attend the party, as they reiterated that Mommy said that they should be able to go to the party. Without hesitation, I told my daughters that my answer is still "No." I attempted to explain that my decision was based on my need to protect them. I don't believe they heard anything except, "No".

This dialogue between the four of us did one thing; it weakened our ability to make parental decisions without our children second guessing us. For me, I was seen as this paranoid dad that wouldn't allow them to have fun; and because I "vetoed" her decision to let them go, Mom didn't have the authority to make decisions in the house. In their eyes, dad is irrational and mom is ineffective and can't influence "Robo-Dad," so they've got to make some decisions. Situations like this and others marked the beginning of the loss of parental control. Children need to hear one answer from both parents. There should be no wiggle room that allows them to think that they have the answers and that mom and dad waver or disagree on what is best for them.

Secondly, because I made my daughters the priority in my life and I focused on keeping their self-esteem high and making them conscious of their self-worth; for a period of time they practiced the "Me, me, me, I, I, and I " way of thinking. If we are not careful, we can create selfish children, and those years of ignoring our marriage and focusing only on our daughters may have caused a rift between my wife and I. This rift caused us to separate and eventually divorce. Sometime after the divorce, I decided to start dating. After dating this one particular woman for several months, I introduced her to my children. At the time my girls were about 6 and 11 years old. My girlfriend also had a daughter who was about 3 years old. I remember talking to my children in hopes of preparing them for this day. We picked my girlfriend and her daughter up and headed to "Disney on Ice" for our first get acquainted event. What happened next was my fault!

After my daughters and I picked my girlfriend and her 3 year old daughter up, I introduced them. After a very uncomfortable exchange of hellos; there was a silence that seemed to last forever. The next words were the smallest of small talk. Thank God for the radio and hallelujah for the volume button to turn it up! I remember looking over at my girlfriend sitting next to me in the passenger seat of my Camero Z28. She had a look on her face I had never seen before. On a couple of occasions I saw her head being drawn back toward her head rest and the slight jerk of her body as though something was forcing her out of her seat. She was either experiencing some supernatural possession or my two little ones positioned directly behind her were up to something. My girlfriend never said a thing and continued to smile through her newly reddened skin tone. I knew something was wrong; I just couldn't place my finger on it at the time.

Disney on Ice was very entertaining and the rest of the evening was uneventful. We grabbed a quick bite to eat and dropped my girlfriend and her daughter off at home. My daughters seemed more excited about saying good night than they did saying hello earlier in the day. I thought maybe they were beginning to accept her, but the loaded smile on my oldest daughter's face suggested something very different.

There are many good reasons to make our children feel that they are a priority and that they are important to us, however; our children must not feel as though their feelings are the only feelings that matter. Therefore, as parents we must create a balance that makes it very clear to our children that others matter and that they must learn to sacrifice sometimes for the sake of others. We often concern ourselves with how well our children are doing in school (IQ), but many of us seldom concern ourselves with our children's emotional intelligence (EI). *Emotional Intelligence,* authored by psychologist Daniel Goleman, is the ability to recognize our own feelings, the feelings of others, and manage those emotions to create strong positive relationships. If we can recognize and own how we may cause others to feel, then maybe many teens won't "pull that trigger." Understanding and valuing emotional intelligence could cause us all to once again see each other as human, breathing, and valuable people that are dearly and wholeheartedly loved by someone. When we teach our young children to not only love themselves, but love and respect the feelings and lives of others, we begin to change life as we know it. Martin Luther King Jr. said it best in a letter from Birmingham Jail, April 16, 1963; "We are caught in an inescapable network of mutuality, tied in a single garment of destiny. Whatever affects one directly, affects all indirectly." So, it is without question that we must love and respect others as we love and respect ourselves. We must teach our children this!

I have more work to do…

The next morning I spoke with my girlfriend and discovered that she was not having a supernatural episode; but that her head was being drawn back toward the headrest by two little hands tugging on her hair. Those hands belonged to my oldest daughter, whom I found out later was displeased with having to share her dad. The slight jerk of my girlfriend's body as though she was being forced out of her seat, well, that was caused by my daughter's four little feet pounding against the back of her chair. I spent so much time attending to their feelings that I didn't spend much time addressing the feelings of others. I quickly learned that I had more work to do. With redirection and an emphasis on emotional intelligence, which I will discuss in depth later in the book, my daughters became more considerate and respectful of the feelings of others. However, it was no easy task. It required that I redirect the way I interact with my children. I set clear guidelines in my mind of those things that were off-limits to their eyes and ears including relationships and discussions among adults that did not concern them. I created a structured day that set clear expectations to include cleaning their room before school, completing homework before asking to play, and asking for permission to do many things they did not need permission to do in the past. I had many more instances where my daughter's would challenge or question occurrences in my life; but empowered with a different way of thinking, I reinforced my newly set guidelines by not discussing issues that were off-limit to their opinions or input and constructively telling them when and why certain comments and opinions by them were not welcomed. I also began to ask my daughter's how they believed they made others feel based on the things they said and did to them. I reminded them how they felt when others had said and done similar things to them. I would help others and say kind things to others in their presence. I believe leading by example is a lasting lesson for our children.

This transformation was challenging, took many months to bring to fruition, but was truly worth it in the long run.

CHAPTER TWO

Effective Parental Involvement

"How to Stay Involved"

Effective parental involvement begins with the parent's state of mind. By "state of mind," I am making reference to our level of consciousness and perception about a particular subject. Specifically, I am referring to what we think about the effects we have on our children on a daily basis. "State of mind" is our belief system about the amount of influence we have over our children. Our children learn from us by what we consciously teach them and from the lessons we teach them subconsciously. We teach our children how to love by how we love. We teach them how to argue by the way we argue in their presence. We are teaching every moment, and they are watching and listening. I remember my father telling me, "Don't do what I do, you do what I tell you to do." That statement is about as frivolous as that rhetorical question, "You want me to whoop your butt again?" In my mind I always thought, "No, duh, I didn't want you to whoop me the first time." Anyhow, our continued effort to remember that we are shaping children and preparing them for the many challenges they will face as young adults is so important. Remember that it's never too late to make changes in how we parent; and as parents it's never too late to mend relationships with an adult son or daughter and take ownership for the past. It may be the acknowledgment of wrongdoing that frees someone you love from the chains of resentment.

Staying involved in the lives of our children is a way of life. It requires us to examine our own lives, because the lives we are living are almost guaranteed to be passed along for generations to come. One of the most difficult aspects of effective parenting is to self-analyze by asking the heart wrenching questions of yourself: Am I a positive role model for my children? Who am I exposing my children to? Are the relationships I place before my children toxic or healthy? Many people destined for self-destruction were rescued by the birth of a child they felt a responsibility to. Alcoholics become non-drinkers, criminals become law-abiding citizens, players find themselves acting like daddies, and divas become mommies.

Sometimes we must change who we are if we are to be successful parents. The changes I am referring to are almost always changes that make us better people in addition to making us better parents.

If I am to get involved in my child's life in a way that is positive, effective, and lasting, I must look at the nesting ground. What kind of environment have I chosen, created, or allowed my child to develop within? These are not often easy assessments to make because it could mean re-evaluating the people I have brought into my life. It could determine the person I choose as a partner because children are involved. Is my current situation conducive to raising children or do adjustments need to be made?

If we are to evaluate our personal lives to benefit our children, to give them the best chance of becoming productive, well-rounded, considerate, and happy individuals; then, we have got to really believe that our sacrifices will make a difference. So, the parent's state of mind is crucial!

As a parent I must:

- ♥ Believe that my involvement is important in my child's development.

- ♥ Believe that I can have a positive effect on my child's development.

- ♥ Have the expectation that my child will be successful.

- ♥ Set standards for my children.

- ♥ Know what tools my child needs to succeed.

- ♥ Be willing and driven by the love for my child to never quit.

How to Stay Involved

We always hear those words, "Stay involved in your child's life." What does that mean and how do I do that?

The Response

"As a matter of fact, I live with my children and I provide for them. You see the clothes they wear, the food they eat, and that roof over their heads? I provide that!"

Although the aforementioned statement is a valid response, we are required by law to provide those things in addition to a few other things. So, what is this involvement that is so connected with the healthy mental development of a child?

No matter what age your child is, there must be stability in your home. Of course, when children are in the early childhood years, this is the best time to create structure for your children. When they are able to understand and follow rules, they should have them. Structure includes standard meal times. At least one meal per day should be distraction free (no cell phones, games, or television) and suitable for open conversation. Stability means that each child should have a bedtime based on the amount of sleep recommended for his/her age. These simple steps seem easy, and they are. The problem is remaining consistent. This might mean you have to pre-plan meals if you work. It might mean you have to get home early on school days. Creating structure for them means that there must be structure for you; at least until they are snug in bed. If your children are older, they must have a curfew, *really* know who their friends are, and require that they share at least one undisturbed meal with the family each day. Children become responsible adults when they are held responsible as children. Cleaning their room is not a chore; it is a requirement to live in your house. There should be no allowance for cleaning your room, picking up after yourself, or putting things back where they belong. However, it is a good idea to give your child additional responsibilities that are to be met at specific times. Requiring your child to wash the dishes, prepare and help with laundry, or collect garbage and place it outdoors on garbage pickup days, teaches them to be responsible. Structure means requiring your children to read and study, but have leisure time as well.

Our children must also develop properly physically; therefore, regular doctor visits, eye examinations, and trips to the dentist are very necessary. In order to comprehend the math problem on the board, the child must be able to see the board. Does my child require glasses? Can my child hear the instructions given to them for a test that will determine their competency?

Not in front of my child!

One of the more difficult things to do is to choose, or lose a mate based on the needs of our children, or the expectation of having children. After all, the heart loves who the heart loves, right? Wrong! The heart loves who we expose the heart to. We must first have expectations for a mate outside of how they look, how they make us feel, the amount of money they have, or "chemistry." If you are already in a relationship and have children, or are considering children with your mate, quickly get this book to your mate. Parenting is best done as a joint venture! Because home is the most effective way to influence a child, we must be strategic about what we place in front of their inquisitive eyes.

If you are in a toxic relationship and you know your partner is no good for you, then they are no good for your child. We as parents teach our children how to disagree by how we disagree. Are we agreeable in disagreeing with others or are we engaging in those "knock down drag out" arguments that bring the police knocking at our door? If the answer to anger is shoving, grabbing, cursing, or hitting; then your child learns that behavior and is prone to repeat it. Needless to say, you are in danger!

Children should see what a healthy relationship looks like. Kind words, affection, consideration, and disagreements that are conversations seeking resolution. Children should witness, "give and take," reciprocity, and mutual respect between you and others you interact with. We should emphasize love and compassion for others in accordance to 1 Corinthians 13:4-7; "Love is patient, love is kind, it does not envy, it does not boast, it is not proud. It does not dishonor others, it is not self-seeking, it is not easily angered, it keeps no record of wrongs. Love does not delight in evil but rejoices with the truth. It always protects, always trusts, always hopes, and always perseveres." We must reinforce these things and that reinforcement may even require limiting or eliminating the time our children spend around those that are not positive role models to include some family members. Everybody's got a crazy uncle, aunt, cousin, brother or sister that set bad examples for our children. We should talk to our children about what behavior is unacceptable.

The goal is to shelter our children from aggressive and violent behavior. But remember, it is never too late to get them away from it either. It could be a life saving decision.

In most cases we are able to seek professional help, sometimes at no charge, when our kids need help overcoming mental sores they are forced to live with. When there are transgressions against our children that are not addressed, those transgressions become "issues" when they are adults. Just think about the number of times you've said, "That girl's got issues!" Well, now you know it very well could have been avoided. When a parent loves a child, only as a parent could do, it is parental instinct to keep that child safe.

True love is healthy and home should feel safe. When we provide a home environment that is free from bickering, free from constant controversy, and free from disorder, we are promoting the healthy development for our children. When there's peace, compassion for one another, and order, home becomes a safe haven from the chaos waiting outside your four walls. Yes, controversy and conflict will emerge, but these are opportunities to teach our children how to value others' opinions, communicate their own opinions, and agree to disagree. We accomplish this by amicably discussing and respectfully resolving conflict in their presence. It is also a good time to communicate to our children that the things we say and do make others feel either good or bad.

We teach our children how to love by requiring that they are nice and polite to others, by helping them to understand that everyone is very precious to someone, and that God wants them to love everyone. If a child understands how precious they are to God and that God loves us all, it is easier for them to love. We must teach our children to not become easily angered and to hate no one. Now more than ever, every child belongs in church.

Are you Stupid or Something?

What we say to our children will either "build them up", or "tear them down." How we talk to them should be age appropriate. We should never use profanity with young children. We should speak in short clear sentences. We should tell our children how proud we are of them, that they are smart, and that we love them. Profanity is never necessary, but when we just have to use it, be sure it is not with the little ones. Remember how they learn to speak. They mock you! If you find yourself always yelling and screaming at your children, they too will become yellers and screamers. As your child gets older we must begin to focus more on creating open lines of communication. We must learn to actively listen to discern what they are saying, respecting that they have opinions, and making them feel comfortable sharing information with us. We must empower them by asking questions that get them thinking and processing information so that they make good choices. At some point we must stop telling them what to do and teach them to "think," because we won't always be there to give them the right answer or tell them how to respond to situations.

Garbage in Garbage out

"The Mind is a terrible thing to waste"

Get your child off of the video games and into a book. Our children spend entirely too much time playing games that simulate killing, carjacking, and other forms of violence. Some people say that it's just a game, but it desensitizes our children to violence. Think about it; when you first heard of a drive-by shooting back in the days of the movie *Colors,* you were devastated that such a thing could happen. Today, we are so immune to violence that we watch it on the news and often feel no emotions about it. We have been desensitized to violence. There is something truly wrong when the object of any game is to earn points for hurting others and committing crime. Make no mistake; the mind is conditioned based on experiences. Real or imagined, it makes our children comfortable with what they should avoid: knowledge in —knowledge out, violence in— violence out. The mind should be processing information that creates a good moral foundation. A moral foundation that teaches our children to respect others, respect themselves, and love their neighbors; not carjack or kill them.

For birthdays or holidays give your children an interesting book that stimulates their minds. Once you know your children's interests, buy them books and equip them with information that gets them hungry to pursue those interests. Video games are not all bad, there just has to be a balance between entertainment and proper stimulation of the minds of our children. There are also games that stimulate children's minds and allow parents to have positive interactions with their children. With a little research on the internet or a visit to your local department store, parents can find a variety of fun games that actually target certain areas of development. An example would be *Word Scramble* for increasing our children's vocabulary, or *Monopoly* which creates the opportunity to develop financial wisdom; and initiate conversations on when to spend, how to spend, and why we should save money.

We can also stimulate our children by helping them to understand their past, where they are from, and why we do the things we do in our culture. This may require that you do your own research first. If we are to embrace and love what we see in the mirror, we must know the depth of our inception. How we got to where we are, what have been our challenges as a people, what makes us great, and what responsibility did we each inherit as a result. If most of our children knew the concept behind the things they do today that are trendy, I strongly believe that they would cease the trend, or in some cases change their behavior to have it match the trends that emerged from something positive.

"Please pull your pants up"

Take the trend of sagging pants, a behavior believed to have originated in the United States Prison System. It dates back to a dress code embraced by criminals, homosexuals, and associated with promiscuity amongst men in the prison system. So, I must ask the question: "Aren't too many of our young black males locked-up already for you guys to be free and still think like a man in prison?" What happened to wanting to be unique, to stand out, or to be original? This type of thinking is similar to the "loose white T-shirts" worn by an overwhelming number of black kids during the summer months. I don't know where this originated from; but what I do know is that several gang members, drug dealers, and others who didn't want to be identified by police told me personally that wearing a white t-shirt allowed them to blend in with others wearing white t-shirts in order to elude the police, or avoid being identified by potential witnesses during or after the commission of a crime. Often witnesses identify suspects of a crime by sharing with local law enforcement the suspect's clothing, height, weight, and direction of travel. This is virtually impossible when everyone is wearing loose fitting white t-shirts. So as a law abiding productive young man, you are asking to not be treated like the people you are emulating. So, I say, "Don't wear a red shirt and khaki pants into a Target store and get upset because customers keep asking you, 'Excuse me, do you work here?'"

Parental Involvement includes:

♥ Establishing stability in your home.

  ✓ Provide safety, nutrition, proper sleep, regular doctor visits and nurturing
  ✓ Expose your children to healthy relationships
  ✓ Shelter your children from aggressive and violent behavior

♥ Using appropriate language.

  ✓ Don't use profanity
  ✓ Avoid screaming and yelling at your child
  ✓ Speak to young children in short clear sentences

♥ Providing the appropriate stimulation to your children.

  ✓ Talk to your children
  ✓ Read often to your children
  ✓ Expose them to a variety of performing arts

♥ Playing educational games that stimulate areas of learning.

♥ Exposing them to history, their heritage, and other cultures.

CHAPTER THREE

Developing Confident, Motivated and Productive Leaders

You can do it!

Stability in the home is the beginning of developing confident, motivated, and productive leaders. In addition to giving our children the confidence to pursue their dreams, the motivation to push through obstacles, and the ability to produce; we want them to be leaders, because leaders tend not to fold as quickly to peer pressure. We want them to feel good about themselves and to dream big. Many great things manifest as a result of a child being confident. We as parents can build our children's confidence by simply telling them that they are smart. If we consistently tell our children that they are unique and special, it creates the image they have of themselves. If we are always asking questions out of anger or agitation like: "Are you stupid, are you an idiot, or Are you dumb?" this is what they start to believe about themselves. If anyone, child or adult, questions whether they are stupid, an idiot or dumb, they surely can't feel good about the person they believe they are. Our self image has little to do with how we really look. Instead, our self image has to do with how we have grown to feel about how we look. We can embrace and love who we are with reinforcement from the one source we trust as a child: our parents. Tell your children that they are beautiful and that being beautiful has more to do with their kindness, consideration, and the respect they have for themselves and those around them.

Positive Exposure

Every child will idolize someone. If we place as many positive role models in their presence as possible, then they are more likely to emulate someone who has great qualities. We want our children in the presence of adults, teens, preteens and other children that are respectful, driven, considerate, positive, caring, patient, slow to anger, and confident.

Encouragement

Every vision began with a dream, and having a vision gives us a reason to have goals, and goals keep us doing positive things.

Encourage your children to dream. When your child tells you that they want to be a doctor, ask them what kind of doctor, and praise the work that doctors do. We can create the energy that fuels their dreams by continuing to encourage them to dream big and by involving them in activities that strengthen their desire to pursue their dreams. Another very effective way to encourage our children is to associate traits and characteristics they possess with those traits and characteristics required to be successful in the endeavors they are choosing to pursue.

So if we are to instill these qualities in our children we must:

- ♥ Tell them that they are smart.

- ♥ Tell them that they are beautiful.

- ♥ Expose them to positive role models.

- ♥ Encourage them to dream.

- ♥ Support their dreams.

Establish a Positive Relationship with Caregivers and Teachers

"Earn your children the benefit of doubt"

Hurry, hurry, rush, rush, the task is to get them to school on time, stop for coffee, and then get to work on time. "Mwah! Love you, see you after school baby." We then hurry off, but who did we just turn our child over to for the next 6-10 hours?

Teachers, educators, principals, deans, resource officers, crossing guards, school counselors, school bus drivers, and any other member of the school's staff all contribute in some way to your child's success and safety when you release them to the care of these figures of authority. What our children believe about these authority figures, as well as the respect or lack of respect for them, could dictate the outcome of situations requiring their intervention.

"Fair or not, it is the truth"

Two children at the same school in the same grade get into similar situations with the same teacher that resulted in two different outcomes of discipline for the two students. On the surface it sounds unfair, but when we look at the intricacies of the two incidents, the two different outcomes make sense. Mike and Terrence are both in the 8th grade and have both got into minor trouble in school. You know the usual; talking when they should be quiet, disrupting the teacher, playing in the hallways, and a couple of fights. However, the particular incidents I want to share involved Mike getting into a fight with an 8th grade student and Terrence getting into a fight with another 8th grade student in two separate incidents. Mike and Terrence initiated and were found to be the aggressors in both fights. The victims of both fights were bruised and scratched in the face area. All of the other information surrounding the incidents was identical except the following: Mike's parents and Terrence's parents approached the parent conferences quite differently.

Mike's parents met with the school's principal. Prior to the principal sharing any of the facts, Mike's mother immediately said to the principal: "Do you have a problem with my son, because he told me that you guys constantly pick on him for no reason at all? I can't keep taking time off work because you can't control your students." Needless to say, there was very little conversation thereafter about correcting Mike's anger issues and his history of fighting. Mike's next fight, which occurred a couple of weeks later, resulted in the school contacting the police and Mike being arrested and petitioned to Juvenile Court; which now gives Mike a criminal record.

Terrence's parents also met with the principal, and thanked him for taking time out of his schedule to meet with them; then the principal explained the details of the fight Terrence was involved in. The principal, Terrence, and Terrence's parents discussed his recent behavior. It was determined that Terrence would attend anger management classes and serve two weekend detentions. The following month, and after two anger management classes; Terrence was involved in another fight. The principal notified Terrence's parents and after a second parent conference with the principal, Terrence was required to attend more frequent anger management classes and served a three day out of school suspension. Terrence was not petitioned to Juvenile Court and did not receive a criminal record.

The moral to this story is that when authority figures and parents are able to work together in the best interest of the child, the child wins. Just as we are all human, so are teachers, principals, police officers, and judges, just to name a few. When authority figures are faced with parents that are just as difficult to deal with as the child in question, it is almost impossible for the authority figure to work with a parent who is approaching the situation being defensive, argumentative, angry, upset or irrational. As a result, authority figures are more likely to refer the child to local law enforcement. If the parent has not, at this point, realized that they need to cooperate with local law enforcement; well, history will repeat itself and local law enforcement is more likely to petition the child to court instead of resolving the issue outside of the criminal court system. It is also good to know that all police departments should have juvenile officers. Juvenile officers are important to the success of "troubled kids" because juvenile officers are specially trained in juvenile law, which is designed to protect children and keep them out of the criminal justice system whenever possible. Parents have more control than they know when it comes to whether or not their child receives a criminal record. Therefore, informed parents are a powerful tool in keeping their children out of the criminal justice system. Later in the book, the legal system and our children will be discussed more in depth.

"Hmm….low B or high C"

Sometimes, there's a thin line as to whether a child receives a grade of *C* or a grade of *B* based on mitigating factors. As an example, Karlissa's cumulative grade in math at the end of the grading period is 79.9 in a 100 point system. Technically this score is a C+. However, throughout the year Karlissa's parents expressed an ongoing interest in Karlissa's success by attending school events, regularly scheduled parent teacher conferences, and during report card pick up day they always discussed with Karlissa's teacher what they could do to help Karlissa improve. Karlissa is an average kid that does what most kids her age do; however, Karlissa has always been respectful towards her teachers. Although Karlissa should have been given a C+, because of the collective effort of Karlissa's family, she received a B as her final grade. Remember that people are human no matter what their occupation may be, and that reciprocity goes a long way. "Work with me, and I will work with you."

So, in establishing a positive relationship with caregivers, teachers, and other authority figures in your child's life, remember to:

♥ Review and discuss homework and projects.

♥ Participate in school functions.

♥ Familiarize yourself with school policies and procedures.

♥ Tell your child the behavior you expect of them before problems arise.

♥ Ask your child about their day and respond with true discernment.

♥ Take a moment and have a conversation with school personnel when you are dropping off or picking up your child in an effort to develop positive relationships at the school.

♥ Handle situations in which you believe your child was treated unfairly responsibly and rationally.

♥ Ask for help if your child needs additional resources to succeed.

♥ Work with the school, not against the school's efforts to teach your child.

♥ Give your child's teacher the means to contact you, (i.e., email, cell phone, or work number).

Remember, do not:

○ Blame, criticize, or disrespect authority in the presence of your child.

○ Justify your child's unacceptable behavior.

○ Expect the school to raise your child. That is not the school's purpose.

EMOTIONAL INTELLIGENCE

"Ask yourself, how would you feel if someone did that to you ?"

Emotional intelligence (EI) is sometimes referred to as emotional quotient or emotional literacy; the term was coined in 1990 by psychologists John Mayer and Peter Salovey. Individuals with emotional intelligence are able to relate to others with compassion and **empathy**, have well-developed social skills, and use this emotional awareness to direct their actions and behaviors. In 1995, psychologist and journalist Daniel Goleman published the highly successful book *Emotional Intelligence*, which was built on Mayer and Salovey's work and popularized the EI concept. You might ask why emotional intelligence is important in how we shape the lives of our children. Well, it is my belief that we have become a selfish world, where everything is mostly about "me." We are raising a generation of children that seek instant gratification, and are seldom concerned about the feelings of others. An example of this behavior is the repulsive increase in bullying, which has caused children to take their own lives because of those who are relentlessly insulting, mean, and sadly unaware of the possible consequences of their actions. It is the carjacking, armed robbery, sexual assault, mob beating, and cold-blooded senseless murder committed by a teen or by a young adult that raises questions as to the mindset of someone who could do such a thing to another human being. In my 21 years of law enforcement, I can't remember an offender ever telling me that they considered the victim's feelings prior to committing a crime. Instead, they were mostly focused on the benefit the crime would produce and decreasing their odds of getting caught. So we know that our children are thinkers; however, we must get them to think right! Although not single handedly, emotional intelligence could be part of the answer. We must begin teaching our children to be more considerate of others so that they don't follow the vicious patterns many of our current day teenagers are choosing; because, make no mistake, the life we live is a choice. Sometimes the choice is more difficult for many because of their environment, parental guidance, or economic status, just to name a few; but the emphasis here: IT IS A CHOICE!

We can boost our children's Emotional Intelligence by adhering to the following:

♥ Remember that video games, TV, and movies may desensitize children to violence; therefore, we should explain that the aforementioned are for entertainment only and limit their exposure to violent forms of entertainment.

♥ Explain to children how their actions make others feel good and/or bad.

♥ Teach them to give back by volunteering at soup kitchens and resale shops, give gifts to the less fortunate.

♥ Teach them to share and to work for what they want by offering them opportunities to earn money for some of the things they want but don't need (i.e. washing your car for money to buy gifts).

CHAPTER FOUR

Gangs, Violence, and our Youth

"Staying Safe in Today's Streets"

The history of street gangs in the United States began as early as 1783 on the East Coast; but, the more serious street gangs are believed to have emerged in the early part of the nineteenth century. So, gangs have been around a while and over time have transformed into something quite different today.

The gang emergence in the Northeast and the Midwest was fueled by immigration and poverty. A large influx of mainly poor white families from Europe arrived in hopes of seeking a better life. However, they had difficulty finding jobs and places to live. In addition, Anglo native-born Americans discriminated against these immigrants. This caused the immigrants to form communities and join each other in the economic struggle.

As gangs emerged, the need for their existence transformed from economic struggle to turf wars or "fighting over territory" and expanding their control. So in essence, gangs began out of the need to survive for the less fortunate; then gradually the gangs would exist out of pure greed.

Today's gangs primarily exist to engage in criminal activity which feeds its members' greed. Illegal drugs, guns, violence, sex trafficking, incarceration and homicides are synonymous with today's gangs. They are responsible for the deaths of many innocent infants, children, women, and men of all ages. It is their presence in areas that have caused communities to become inhabitable and the value of homes to decrease. Gangs are more than a problem; they are an epidemic that has taken more lives than some wars on record. Let there be no mistake; because of gangs, we are at war right here in our own front yards.

In part, to win the war against gangs we must prevent their growth by keeping our kids gang-free and safe as the war on gangs is fought. Although many would agree that gangs need to be eradicated and wiped from the face of the earth like the plague they are; that task is difficult because of the gang's widespread reach and the fear it brings with it. Until we win the war against gangs, we must use every tool at our disposal to keep our children, families, and communities safe from the gang's destruction. Staying safe from gangs is like avoiding a tornado. It's kind of like knowing what a tornado looks like, understanding the path it frequently travels, remembering the catastrophe it leaves behind, and then making the conscious decision to stay out of its path. To keep our children safe in today's streets we must understand what gangs look like. Knowing that gangs normally identify with a dominant color, tattoo, hand gesture and handshake makes you aware of them. You may see them hanging in groups, hats clearly cocked to one side, bandannas, and team jackets; like the New Orleans Saints jacket which has a symbol resembling a three-pronged pitchfork symbol which is synonymous with the Folk Nation Alliance. This is just the tip of the iceberg, but by no means is this a lesson in gang identification. Instead, this intended to raise awareness; so that we may help our children avoid the destructive trail that these vicious groups of criminals tend to leave behind. However, unlike a tornado which comes and goes, these gangs seem to never go away; they just change faces, names, and generations, but with the same purpose. That purpose is to kill, steal, and destroy. To sum it up; gangs are defined as two or more people whose purpose is to engage in criminal activity.

"Something is different about you"

As parents, we have an instinct that tells us when something is not right with our children. Sometimes we can't quite put our finger on it, but find ourselves telling our children, "Something is different about you." Well, when it comes to behavior changes that indicate that our children may be involved in gang activity or interested in becoming a gang member, there are a few consistent indications.

- ♥ Changes in appearance – Wears only one or two colors of clothing exclusively

- ♥ Takes on a nickname / Hand signs also known as stacking

- ♥ May have unexplained bruises or cuts

- ♥ Possesses a weapon

- ♥ Possesses unexplained cash and expensive items

- ♥ Hanging out late /drug paraphernalia found in their room

- ♥ Missing medicine (valium, vicodin, cough syrup)

- ♥ Withdraws from family functions or old friends

- ♥ Refuses to allow parents to meet new friends

- ♥ Finds trouble at school and with the police

Each of the aforementioned behaviors alone may not indicate anything about our children, but when two or more of these behaviors occur together, it is time for us to get concerned and intervene.

"The Aftermath"

R.I.P.

Gangs are synonymous with violence, destruction, jail, and death. Despite these known facts, children still join them. The million dollar question is....... Why?

Why do children join gangs?

Understanding why children join gangs provides us with an additional tool in the fight against gangs and decreases the chances of our children being enticed by gangs. Yes, enticed! Contrary to what many people believe, children today are seldom forced into gangs. Children are "born into gangs," join for protection, a feeling of belonging, or they are enticed by the the perceived easy money and good times.

Born into Gangs

"It's the only life I know"

A few years ago I had a conversation with a young man who had been incarcerated most of his teenage and young adult life. He was first incarcerated when he was only 13. This was his story!

From the cradle to the grave, it's the only life I know. In the first pictures I remember seeing of myself, I was in my crib and surrounded by semi-automatic weapons. Both of my ears were pierced before I was out of pampers. I was taught that respect is earned by setting an example so others would never have the courage to disrespect my family, and that anyone who had the courage to disrespect our name never got a second chance to do so again. Certain penalties were final and irreversible. My dad was a lifelong gang member, his dad was a lifelong gang member, and my mother and grandmother alike knew the rules and followed status quo. The gang is my life. I don't know any other way to live. I have lost count of the many funerals I have attended because we lost family. We expect that we can be wiped off the face of the earth on any given day, but once you are in the game as deep as we are, death is the only way out. Sometimes I get tired of the death and violence all around me and I have had moments where I wanted to get out, but I know that means relocating everyone I care about and changing my identity. Sometimes I get angry that I didn't have a choice, and that I didn't have the option to have a normal family, true friends, and maybe go to college. I would have maybe pledged a fraternity or took acting classes. There have been times when the gang comes before my family because the gang is family. Although many of my values were taught by the gang, deep down inside I felt loyalty to my biological family because I could feel how much my mom and dad truly loved me. I never felt that connection from my gang family. In fact, my feelings were reinforced about family when a member of the gang family was executed by our gang family because he was a threat to the family. He was only 15.

I'm in too deep now, I will die living this life; either on the street or in the joint (prison).

I reflected on this young man's story and decided to share it because I am hoping children will learn from his story that a gang's promise to provide the things we get from our family (i.e. love, support, guidance, and a sense of belonging) is just a promise of an early death or loss of freedom. Unfortunately, there are thousands of stories just like his.

"Everything you should get at home"

Safety, Security, Acceptance, Guidance, and Love

Home is known to be the training ground that shapes and molds us for the lives we will live. Our values, morals, belief systems, and self-perception are all affected by what happens within the home. Home is where we learn how to love, how to respect others, and how to forgive. When I speak of home, I am speaking of the family dynamics within the home. The family dynamic is how family members relate to one another; and the most important relationship in the home is that of parents to their children. This relationship is most important because when parental nurturing is absent, risk factors for gang involvement increase. To lessen the chance of our children wanting to join a gang, it's important to know what family risk factors attribute to children wanting to join a gang. The most prevalent are below.

Family Risk Factors

- Poor parental supervision and control

- Lack of love and affection in the home

- Not feeling a sense of belonging

- Family poverty

- Family transitions

- Child abuse and neglect

Let's explore each of the Family Risk Factors

Poor parental supervision and control

At the age of 22, my oldest daughter said to me during a conversation, "Daddy, I'm glad that you were a strict father."

When I asked her what she meant, she explained that there were a lot of things she really wanted to do as a child and that although she begged she was actually relieved when I would say no. She gave me an example of a time when she wanted to go to a party with friends, but I told her no because I was aware that the party had no parental supervision and I didn't know the friends who were having the party. She didn't share with me at the time but 6 years later she would tell me that friends of hers experienced alcohol and drugs for the first time at that party, and that some of those girls became repeated users and were pregnant by the age of 17. I tell you this to say, children want structure, they want rules, and they need to hear the word "no" as much as they need to hear "yes, that's okay." When we give our children curfews and hold them accountable for adhering to those curfews, chores, expected grades and conduct in school, we are teaching them to live with structure. When children understand structure, expectations, and accountability they learn to exercise discipline and embrace the power to say no, even under peer pressure. As a parent, don't be afraid to bend less when it comes to creating structure and accountability in your child's life.

Lack of love and affection in the home

Creating a connection with our children can create a closeness that keeps the lines of communication open and sends the message to our children that they matter and that we care. Imagine, even as an adult, when we are around people that acknowledge our presence and make us feel that they like us; we want to be around them, we tend to trust them, and we want to please them because they please us. When we make that type of connection with our children, they want to please us and it gives us an additional tool in keeping them away from gangs and people that may be harmful to them.

Connections are created when we hug our children, hold them, and tell them that we love them. Just as we remember the people that compliment us, our children remember when we tell them how great they are. A smile and encouragement can build the foundation that reminds your child that nowhere is better than home.

Not feeling that they belong

If children feel displaced in their own home, they will eventually seek a sense of belonging somewhere else. Well, what makes a child feel displaced? As an adult what makes us feel like we aren't wanted in a particular place? Perhaps being ignored, made to feel that you are, "in the way," or maybe that you have no purpose. Feeling invisible can make anyone simply want to disappear. So how do we make our children feel that home is where they belong? I believe it starts with making them feel involved and safe at home by ensuring that home is a positive environment. We can make them feel involved by praising them for helping to maintain an orderly home through their daily chores. We can also make them feel that they belong by creating positive memories in the home (e.g., holiday traditions, birthday parties, fun interactive games). Positive reinforcement could be simply telling your child that you love having them around.

Family poverty

A gang member may befriend a child by buying that kid a popular pair of gym shoes or a piece of clothing that we as parents may not be able to afford. A gang may entice a child by wearing fashionable clothing, driving flashy cars, and offering ways to help your child earn money to purchase those things. Well, we know what that means; they want your child to participate in the gang's drug trafficking and other illegal activities. We must teach our children to not praise material things, but to honor the law, to work for the things that they want, and instill in them the concept behind, "Easy come easy go."

Family transitions

Children may be affected by changes in the family structure. Divorce, blended families, incarceration of a parent, or consistent absence from the home by of one or both parents can alter a child's behavior. The thing to remember in any of these situations is that the child's welfare cannot take a back seat to the issues that may be overwhelming to the parents because when we decrease the attention we give our children, we increase the attention they are open to receive from others. Unfortunately, "others" tend to be gangs or other children who are delinquent.

Child abuse and neglect

Needless to say, children who are neglected or abused tend to feel alienated and for obvious reasons may distance themselves from the abuser and find comfort, security, and peace outside of the home.

CHAPTER FIVE

Avoiding Gangs

"Bring your A Game"

So, when we have eliminated as many of the family risk factors as possible, ensuring that our children, "Bring their A Game" is our next order of business. We can avoid gangs by the choices we make in our:

- ♥ Appearance

- ♥ Affiliation

- ♥ Attitude

Appearance

"What's on the outside, counts as much as what's on the inside"

In a training exercise I conducted with students from ages 8 through 18, parents, and teachers, the participants were asked to look at a photograph of a person and make an observation.

The participant's observations of the person in the photograph were literally unanimous. The image was a male wearing a blue and white baseball cap slightly tilted on his head, a blue wave cap (du-rag), a plain white t-shirt, and a long silver chain with a star emblem.

My first question to the participants: "What do you believe he does for a living, what is his occupation?" In each of the nearly 50 training exercises I conducted, the following were standard replies:

➢ "He doesn't have a job"

➢ "Thug"

➢ 'Gangbanger"

➢ "Drug dealer"

➢ "Oh my God, he's probably got a gun"

Although, "you can't judge a book by its cover," this exercise made it very clear that "perception can be reality;" and although an individual may be a person of great character, the person people perceive that individual to be can be an invitation to mistreatment. I do understand that this may not be fair, but we are living in dangerous times and my goal is to keep our children safe during our fight to end the senseless killing of our children. We must teach our children to dress for their roles in life. Until the world understands that the substance of a man cannot be judged by how he dresses or presents himself to the world, we must teach our children to not be mistaken as one of those lost souls that work against God's purpose for us as a people.

How we present ourselves to the world, our image, can be an invitation to mistreatment by society, negative attention by gang members, and violence. Some may argue that our children have the right to dress, speak, and behave the way they choose, and I agree; however, exercising that right should not supersede the opportunity to lessen the chance of a child becoming another statistic. As a parent, I would not allow my children to dress in clothing that even hinted to the world that they were thugs. Like it or not perception is reality to the person interacting with your child. We tell the world who we are everyday; but more importantly, who are we telling them we are?

Are you dressing for your role in life?

Our children should dress for success. How we look effects how we feel, and how we feel effects how we behave. The sagging pants, underwear on display and hoodie with an ungroomed head of hair creates a different energy than a groomed young man with a buttoned-up shirt and slacks worn on the waist. Appropriately presenting ourselves to the world generates a sense of pride and self worth within us. When a young man or a young lady encounters someone in an everyday situation, what one sees before them is their first impression of that young lady or young man. How others view us determines how they treat us. Whether it's an interview for a job, or an encounter requiring someone to trust us, their first impression could be a lasting impression. How people treat us effects what we think of ourselves.

Furthermore, attire associated with gang membership could cost an innocent child his or her life because opposing gangs often shoot without asking questions. Also, gangs who think a child is false flagging, pretending to be a member of their gang, may be beaten or shot as well.

Attire associated with negativity can also attract negative attention from the authorities. I want to speak on the negativity associated with the "hoodie." The hoodie is known to be used as a way for offenders to conceal their identities during the commission of crimes. Hoodies were worn during bank robberies, armed robberies, and sexual assaults; we have all seen these videos on the local news. Although suspicion is no reason to harass anyone, whenever someone appears to be concealing their identity, we all get a little nervous. Stop your children from wearing hoodies because so many criminals are using them for wrongdoing.

There are just so many reasons to dress differently and separate oneself from life's menaces to society. The sooner we direct what our children can and can't wear, the easier it is to teach them to dress for success. If your children are older, appeal to them as a concerned parent who cares about their safety.

Remember: A negative image can be an invitation to:

✓ Violence

✓ Mistreatment

✓ Negative attention

"A *Good name is rather to be chosen than great riches, and loving favour rather than silver and gold" **Proverbs: 22:1**

In furtherance, some children may spend time with kids that are involved in gang and criminal activity. Explain to your children that affiliation can be as deadly and dangerous as being a gang member or taking part in crime. Unfortunately, perception can become another's reality.

"If it walks like a duck, quacks like a duck...
It's a duck"

"Make no friends with an angry man:
and with a furious man thou shalt not go"
Proverbs 22:24

Growing up we encounter individuals that we consider our friends. We often attend the same school, live in the same community, or are related to those we choose to spend time with. There are many variations of what friendship means to all of us, but one thing that a friend should not be is a distraction or danger to our well-being. I understand that it may be difficult to part ways with someone we have grown comfortable being around, or simply enjoy hanging out with; however, the people we knew as kids may have grown up to be people with very different life aspirations than we have. It may also be that we are as guilty as that acquaintance that brings out the worst in us. Either way, they are fuel to the fire and may hinder our ability to avoid trouble. No matter how much we care about our friends, we should never love our friends more than we love ourselves. We were all made in God's image; and as a reflection of God, who is love, we should love ourselves. So:

➤ When childhood friends begin to make bad choices - let them go.

➤ When new friends seem to be traveling a troubled path – let them go.

➤ When girlfriends or boyfriends seem to attract or create negative energy – let them go.

➤ If you find yourself in the company of gangbangers – "You know-it's time to go!"

Consider this: "guilty by association" and "being in the wrong place at the wrong time" have contributed to the loss of freedom (incarceration) for the innocent, negative attention, unsolicited violence, and death.

Attitude

*Life is… **10%** what happens to us and **90 %** how we respond*

Translation: We have nearly absolute control of our lives when we make good choices regarding the 10% we can't control.

Attracting Positive Associations

How we deal with the things that happen to us is just as important as *what* happens to us. Being a positive person for some is an innate behavior. For others it is a learned behavior that when practiced becomes a habit and eventually becomes who they are. It is important that we as parents learn to dwell on the sunny side of life when possible, and teach our children to look at the brighter side of life, see the good in others, and enjoy what is great about life without discounting the fact that we can't be naive about life. We are all a representation of energy; that is, we create the environment we live in by how we treat others. If we are loud, obnoxious, rude, or confrontational, we attract others who exhibit that behavior as well. We are, however, not likely to attract positive attention from those who are kind, considerate, or caring if we are not. Love is the antidote to hatred. So we must teach our children how to love others. Our children must understand that how we treat others is how we will be treated. How others treat us effects how we view ourselves.

Love in Action

So, we should encourage our children to:

- ♥ Practice self love–love themselves by acknowledging what is great about themselves

- ♥ Be kind to others in how they speak to them and respect the feelings of others in a way that says they are important

- ♥ Appreciate affection - hug them

- ♥ Perform acts of kindness - volunteer

- ♥ Say kind encouraging things to others

- ♥ Avoid negative talk

Intervention and Prevention

A Parent's Checklist

♥ Maintain an open and honest relationship with your children

♥ Encourage them to develop a positive relationship with a trusted adult at school

♥ Emphasize that they avoid contact with troublemakers / gangbangers

♥ Remind them to never play tough if confronted

♥ Tell them that if they are approached to remain non-confrontational, Prayer has been known to persuade the adversary to back down

♥ Keep a positive attitude – Honor what God requires of us; get to know God, honor their parents, love themselves, and love others

♥ Discourage your children from hanging around with gang members

♥ Occupy your children's free time / know and support their interests

♥ Develop good communication with your children

♥ Spend time with your children

♥ Be your teen's biggest fan!

♥ Do not buy or allow your child to dress in gang-styled clothing

♥ Set limits for your children – curfew/rules / chores

♥ Establish a rapport with the staff at your child's school

♥ When necessary, contact the Gangs Unit of your local law enforcement agency for guidance and assistance

Remember: Children should have a limited expectation of privacy.

Attitude toward Elders and Authority

Equip them with self-respect, knowledge, discipline and an agenda

We must learn to be more informed as people and understand that the very freedom we use to disrespect our elders is a freedom our elders suffered and died for with our well-being in mind. It is ironic and heartbreaking to perpetuate a cycle that will someday position all of us as elders at someone's mercy. It will be this understanding that will take us back to the times when we avoided use of profanity in the presence of our elders; and we protected the weakened and dependent elders in some respect. We looked into their eyes and saw their struggles, their wisdom, and became hungry for their knowledge; not their belongings. Because we loved and respected the elders in our family, we assumed that someone had to love and respect those elders who were not our family. For this reason, we too respected them. I encourage children to spend time with their elders to learn from their journeys, grow from their experiences, and be encouraged by their triumphs. This will begin the process of re-establishing the elder's as the honorable, respected, and protected members of society they deserve to be.

CHAPTER SIX

The Black Community, the Police, & the Truth

"Living one more day to take one more step toward King's Dream"

Death is such a final cost to pay to make a point. In addition, there's a very detrimental question we must ask ourselves: How do we fight the "right" fight? We can go on and on since as early as we can remember, and call out the names of those that we believe died at the hands of injustice. We often hear three perspectives as to what occurred. We hear the involved officer's view, the witness or bystander, and the media's view; all of which are obscured in some way. More importantly, it is important to carefully filter views presented by the media. The media is the biggest proponent of drama, the diva of partial truths, and the architect of the ongoing tension building between the Black Community and the Police. Remember, the media, aka "your local news," needs an audience. We, the audience, will stop in our tracks to hear controversy, stories of injustice, and scandals. The media knows that drama and controversy draws an audience and the success of their network is based on the number of viewers they attract. So, it makes sense that the media would present the most dramatized version of the story. Stories told by an onlooker whose account of the incident is unconfirmed are often reported. Truths are stretched to entertain the audience and the well-being of society takes a back seat. Therefore, we must become informed by other means than the media alone. In a world with the internet, information is available at the click of a button. Laws, local ordinances, use of force protocol, as well as the burden of proof required to convict an officer who may have abused his authority, or a civilian who may have broken the law are readily available for your educated and informed view. Knowledge is powerful and if we are to become involved in the societal woes that plague us, we must come prepared to fight with the truth, and when we find that the truths are not fair and equitable, we assemble to make change. In our quest to make change, we must be prepared to **Fight the Right Fight**. The Right Fight begins with:

✓ Knowing the facts and reserving judgment until factually informed.

✓ Understanding how the law works and the legislation that speaks to our concerns.

✓ Assembling and sending a powerful message to our elected officials demanding change.

✓ Being an informed voter and holding elected officials accountable.

✓ Peacefully demonstrating and lobbying for action.

"White Police Officer shoots another unarmed Black youth"

Fighting the Right Fight is what we must do because there is already a system in place to eradicate injustices. We can make that system work if we unite in the masses with a powerful message and demand a course of action. Whether we are talking about cops allegedly killing unarmed innocent children, racial profiling, or other behaviors that violate an individual's Constitutional Rights, we must act. We must learn to challenge the legislature and current practices that work against the general welfare and well being of the people, and not waste our time and jeopardize our lives challenging those who are assigned to enforce the legislature and current practices. Take for instance the officer's *use of force* paradigm. The paradigm in Illinois justifies the officer in using deadly force, including death, if the offender's actions are likely to cause great bodily harm or death to the officer or another. THE

OFFENDER DOES NOT HAVE TO BE ARMED WITH A FIREARM OR OTHER DEADLY WEAPON.

REAL COMMUNITY POLICING

Mending a damaged relationship

There is a responsibility on the behalf of the police and the community to change the current relationship between the two groups. The community needs policing and the police need the community to fight the ever growing crime in our neighborhoods. Make no mistake, there is a war going on, and whether you like it or not, YOU ARE IN THE WAR. The war is a war on crime. It is the forever deep desire of every breathing human being to feel safe. We all want to feel our loved ones are safe and that every child has the opportunity to grow-up. Whether you have children or not, you may have nieces, nephews, or a neighbor's kid you have grown to care about. If neither of these relationships exists in your life; consider that someday you will not be the strong self sufficient, "I got this, I can take care of me," person you are today. If we are all blessed to become elderly, and that is the goal — to grow old, we will need to depend on those we *should* be cultivating now. So, all of us should be investing in the strength of our community. A strong community must have structure. Structure means that our communities must have order and rules to ensure that that order is adhered to. We have rules, and they are called laws. Those laws are a binding custom of practices that are enforced by a controlling authority. That authority is the police. Police, in essence, exist to serve the community. Yes, POLICE ARE SERVANTS OF THE COMMUNITY. Police are the enforcing authority performing under oath to keep peace and order as set forth in the laws passed by representatives who were elected by the voting community to be their voice. In other words, as a voting community we have access to change the things we don't believe serve the greater good of the community.

So, how do we change the quarrelsome relationship that exists between the Black community and the police? Well, how does a relationship "go bad" and how do we develop "good relationships" in everyday interactions with others? The answer is that past interactions create future expectations and only a consistent pattern of change over time can create a different expectation. Familiarity creates comfort, and comfort can promote trust. The Black community has experienced a disproportionate number of injustices at the hands of the police as compared to other races. These injustices have been proven over and over again in a court of law, yet the Black community has yet to feel equality under the law. There is much to be done on behalf of police departments to eliminate the inequities and develop a productive relationship with the Black community, and all citizens for that matter.

"Fighting the right fight to fight another day"

Our feelings of inequality are justified; but the approach to resolution by many has been unproductive and tragic. We must teach our young community that their fight is not on the street with every cop they encounter. Most cops are fair and operate according to the law; however, for the few that blemish the badge, we should resist their behavior, and fight their prejudices in a court of law and not on the streets of our communities. When our youth find themselves having to interact with the police, teach them to comply with the officer's requests, remain objective, and non-argumentative. Our youth must understand that they may be good, law-abiding, non-violent kids, and may not pose a threat to an officer that has approached them; but the officer only knows what is presented to them at that moment. When an officer is met with resistance, they become as alarmed for their safety as the person who has been approached and things sometimes quickly get out of control. We want our youth to be safe. Officers who are operating under the law are trained to allow the person(s) they encounter to "Dictate the officer's actions." It's important to know that officers are taught that they are justified to use a specific amount of force based on the other person's actions. What is important about this is that if the officer is conducting his or herself according to the law, they are ONLY to react to the actions of the person. When officers do not conduct themselves according to the law, we must report their actions to the independent agencies established to investigate alleged wrongdoings of the police. We should follow through with the investigation as a community and demand justice. If we find that the officer acted within the law and there is still an injustice in the matter, we should challenge the law that gave the officer the right to respond in the manner. Be prepared to prove that the officer's action was unjust. Likewise, be sure that we consider our actions in the matter. We are all responsible for mending the relationship between the police and the community.

Community Policing

"Belief systems dictate behavior"

We are all a product of our family beliefs, traditions, environment, education, or lack thereof. It is our exposure to other cultures, as well as what we experienced and were told about other cultures. We cannot be held accountable for the aforementioned, but we must all be accountable for our actions regardless of the ignorance that may have been taught to us. Accountability begins with changing our mindset because, "For as a man thinks, so is he " (Proverbs 23:7 KJV).

Everything we do originates in the mind. How we feel about someone is effected by what we think of them. So in essence, feelings begin as a thought. The mind has control over the heart. We as human beings tend to fear what we don't know and favor what we have become familiar with. Our communities need true community policing. Police must have interactions with the communities they serve that are genuine and ongoing. Many police departments pride themselves on having a paramilitary presence. Today's present situation requires more emotional intelligence on behalf of the police and less of a military approach. The community must experience the human aspect of police personnel.

Most people are law abiding, productive, hard-working citizens and deserve to feel protected from the scum of the earth. At this critical point in time, everyone should want peace, justice, and communities that are safe. That includes the community and the police; therefore, we must find a common ground to stand upon and collectively neutralize those who defy the law, threaten the safety and well-being of our families, and destroy the neighborhoods we live in. The community will have to share information with the police and the police will have to earn the communities trust back.

Residents must reach across the table, engage in dialogue and become instrumental in creating safer neighborhoods. If the police are talking to everyone, the bad guys can't truly enforce their campaign that, "snitches get stitches," because everybody is talking to the police, except the bad guys, of course. Remember when police officers were seen as heroes? Officer Friendly was loved because he was one of the good guys. One bad officer does not speak to the many officers that will and have sacrificed their lives, because that's the job. We have to get back to the business of a community and police partnership that works for us all. That change begins with creating trust through everyday interactions by both the community and the police. Police need training in aspects of emotional intelligence, and the community must begin the process of forgiveness. After all, generally speaking, good officers are being judged by what a few bad officers have done. Accountability should be from top leadership down. For accountability, maybe chiefs, commanders, or superintendents of police departments should be elected instead of appointed, just a thought. We must consider these things so that we leave our children a better world than we inherited, and simultaneously we must diligently work to prepare our children so that they are worthy of maintaining and securing a better future for their children.

CHAPTER SEVEN

Parenting is not a friendship

"Yes, doing what's right for them isn't easy"

It is a natural feeling to want our children to like and accept us; but if we are not careful we can lose sight of what is necessary to properly prepare them for life.

The goal is to have our children respect us, and that is very different from liking us.

One of the more difficult tasks of parenting is to address issues with our children that make us feel as though we're being confrontational or invading their privacy. If you're the type of person that feels awkward during these times, take a deep breath and relax, you're not alone and it's okay to have these feelings. No one ever said that parenting was easy, but watching a child you love self destruct is harder.

I always follow a couple of rules during these times. First, I ask myself what's the purpose and goal of the conversation that I'm about to have with my child. Remember conversation means to talk and listen! Be sure to not punish your child for being honest; however, we must still hold them accountable for their actions when necessary. Secondly, I want my child to be honest and open to discussing the subject, so I must ask an open-ended question that is not accusatory, judgmental, or challenging.

Whose weed is this?

A great example would be finding marijuana in your child's bedroom while cleaning. Although it may have upset you, it's important to choose a time to talk with your child that is appropriate. Although the issue should be discussed as soon as practical, doing so with a calm head and a game plan will make a world of difference. In determining the purpose and goal of addressing the issue, the purpose could be to find out why your child is in possession of marijuana and if your child is using marijuana. The goal of the conversation could be to emphasize to your child the dangers of using illegal drugs and that the use of illegal drugs will not be tolerated. Whether your child is experimenting and able to just stop smoking marijuana or a user who may need help, your response will determine the next steps. It is important to create dialogue between you and your child and avoid lecturing because you will need the answer to several other questions like, why and when they began smoking marijuana, as well as where they got it. These and other relevant questions may need answering to begin correcting your child's misstep.

Once you have determined the purpose and goal of the conversation, you must now determine how to open the conversation in a way that will encourage your child to engage in the conversation. In this situation I might preface my question in a calm voice with, "I value our ability to be open and honest with each other and there is nothing we can't get through together. I am concerned about something I found in your closet while putting your bed linen away and I would like for us to talk about it. I found marijuana on the shelf in your closet. Have you tried smoking marijuana?"

Remember, there is no perfect way to have difficult conversations, but consider what has helped your child to have an honest and open conversation in the past, and the aforementioned rules. Although we must have an open dialogue with our children and we should speak in a manner that promotes their input, your understanding, patience, and concern for their well being should not promote leniency when it comes to discipline for their behavior. Whether your form of punishment is to deny your child certain privileges, time outs, spankings, lecturing, or positive reinforcement; I say, "Let the punishment fit the crime." In other words, the punishment should make sense.

Here are a few good parenting tips:

- ♥ Look around you

- ♥ Sneak and snoop

- ♥ Talk to your kids about what you have observed

- ♥ Don't be confrontational, be understanding

♥ Question unexplained money and expensive items

♥ Don't be afraid to ask them embarrassing questions.

♥ Ask to meet their friends

♥ Monitor internet and phone activity

♥ Know with whom and where your kids are at all times

♥ Get help when necessary from trusted family members, local law enforcement, community groups, or your church family

♥ Expect that disciplining and setting guidelines for our children may sometimes be more difficult for us than it is for our children; but it is very necessary

♥ The lesson we teach them today, no matter how difficult it is for us, is the lesson that will save them later

CHAPTER EIGHT

The Legal System and Our Children

"For or Against us"

Contrary to what we may believe, Juvenile Law is designed to protect our children. It offers our children an alternative to jail. It is known that a child's level of maturity and lack of good judgment is mostly a temporary thing, and that as the average child matures and experiences life, they will become more responsible and make better decisions. Although our children know right from wrong, they still sometimes make bad choices and that will normally change over time. For that reason, they should be afforded the opportunity to live productive lives as adults and free of criminal histories, whenever possible. Our legal system recognizes this and therefore has a legal system specifically designed to address juvenile delinquency.

The juvenile legal system has given parents and law enforcement a way to keep our children free of a criminal history as adults when they violated the law as minors. However, there are a few things that must be considered by law enforcement when contemplating whether to charge a juvenile for violating the law. Some of the considerations include: the seriousness of the crime, the juvenile's past violations, school attendance and effort, and the child's attitude.

One of the most important aspects of law enforcement's decision to charge the juvenile criminally or not is the ATTITUDE of the PARENTS. I can explain it better in these two scenarios inspired by many true stories.

Two students involved in very similar situations may have a different outcome based on the parent's approach to the situation.

Scenario #1 – Jacksen, who is in the 6th grade, was caught in school with a pocket knife, which is considered to be a weapon and against school policy. Upon notifying Jacksen's parents, they immediately responded to the school. After hearing the facts as to what occurred, Jacksen's parents asked Jacksen to explain where he got the knife and why he brought the knife to school. Jacksen explained that he saw the camping knife in his dad's tool box and that after playing with the knife he put the knife in the jacket that he wore to school and that he forgot that the knife was in his pocket. Jacksen's parents explained to him that he must follow the rules of the school and that it was his responsibility to not bring prohibited items to school and that he should apologize to the administrator for his mistake. Jacksen did sincerely apologize and was released with a warning to not do it again.

Scenario #2 – Marland, who is also in the 6th grade, was caught in school with a pellet gun, which is considered to be a weapon and against school policy. Upon notifying Marland's parents, they immediately expressed their disgust in the school's inability to handle their students. Marland's parents informed the school that they were at work and that this minor school problem would just have to wait. Eventually, Marland's mother, Janet, agreed to come to the school. Janet never allowed the school or Marland to explain what had happened; instead, she suggested that her son was being targeted by the school and wanted to know why her son's backpack had been searched by the security officer. When the principal explained that another student had seen Marland with the pellet gun and reported him to the principal's office, Janet yelled at the principal asking, "You mean you people called me off work for a toy gun!" The local police were notified and an officer intervened because Janet had become irate. After the police officer was informed of the situation, the officer took Marland to the police station, accompanied by Janet.

Once at the police station, the officer informed Janet that he was a juvenile officer. The officer explained that being a juvenile officer meant that he was well versed in juvenile law and that he needed to ask her a few questions to determine the course of action they would take regarding the pellet gun Marland had brought to school. The officer then asked Janet a series of questions about Marland's school grades, previous run-ins with law enforcement, and if he followed rules at home. Janet became defensive and asked the officer what her rules at home had to do with the school situation. The officer began to explain that he and Marland's parents could work together to help Marland through this situation. Janet interrupted the officer and said, "My husband and I don't need your help raising our son, I think you guys are making a big deal out of nothing and I want to get a lawyer to continue this conversation."

The officer then decided to petition Marland to juvenile court for Unauthorized Possession of a Weapon, and as a result a criminal arrest appeared on Marland's record which required him to appear before a judge in criminal court as an offender.

These are two very similar incidents with very different outcomes. So, what's the moral to these stories? As parents we have more control than we know when it comes to whether or not our children receive a criminal record.

Juvenile officers can choose to handle juvenile delinquency with an Informal Station Adjustment, a Formal Station Adjustment, or Petition the child to Juvenile Court.

Informal and Formal Station Adjustments are agreements between the Juvenile Officer and the parents of the juvenile. The agreement normally entails the child refraining from the activity that got him or her in trouble, going to school and maintaining passing grades, completing house chores, and adhering to curfew. If the child adheres to the agreement for the specified time, the child will not be charged with the crime, keeping them clear of a criminal record. If the juvenile and their parents are uncooperative, it leaves the officer with one choice: charge the child criminally and send them before a judge.

Therefore; an informed parent is a powerful tool in keeping a child out of the criminal justice system.

CHAPTER NINE

Staying Focused

"Helping our children overcome disruptions"

"All that I ask you to do is to go to school, stay out of trouble, and pass your classes! That's not much to ask!" Sorry, my fellow parent, it's easier said than done considering all the distractions our children face. Even the most disciplined children will face peer pressure, temptation, and other forces working against them. In order to keep our children focused and productive, we must anticipate the distractions that exist.

Distractions are defined as something that takes your attention away from what you're supposed to be doing. I like to take this definition a little further by adding that distractions become obstacles in the path of our children's success. Once we are conscience of these distractions, we have a better opportunity to prepare our children to avoid them before they emerge.

Some examples of distractions are:

Friends: Not every friend in your child's life will have been taught the morals, values and dreams you have instilled in your child. Most bad advice our children receive, they get from a peer.

Family: Although we love our family, we must put our child's well-being first. Many times it is the people closest to us that our children learn from. It is the people closest to our children that they pick up habits from. Sometimes we prohibit our children from being friends with other children that are bad influences, but we allow them to spend time with cousins and other family members who are just as bad. Just remember that a bad influence is a bad influence no matter who it comes from. However, if you're able to reverse the bad behavior of the family member, well then do just that.

Relationships: When our children become interested in having girlfriends or boyfriends, we must begin having those conversations that give them a good foundation. Shockingly, this will become an issue long before you believe they should date; however, your belief does not stop hormone activity. Although you may require them to wait some years, they will still find others attractive. For this reason we must talk with our children about our expectations and set reasonable boundaries so that you as a parent are involved in this very crucial time in their lives. They will need guidance so that they don't neglect their school work because they're daydreaming about "the loves of their lives." Unfortunately, some children also experience abuse at the hands of a partner as early as the teen years. Our children are also experimenting with sex at an earlier age. Many kids have their first sexual experience during grammar school. Whether they are touching, kissing, or actually engaging in sexual intercourse, it's very important that we understand that relationships can be a distraction. This type of distraction can result in pregnancy, which is a distraction for many years to come. We must be present to prevent this type of distraction in their lives. The best prevention for relationship distractions is to promote open communication with your child by being:

✓ Non-Judgmental – Listening without scolding

✓ A good listener – Encouraging them to share more information by showing empathy *(Remember, you were once a kid!)*

✓ Empathetic – Asking and allowing them to suggest what you were going say (this requires that you have the skills to lead them to the right answer). It's easier for them to digest and follow their own advice.

✓ Firm in setting guidelines and expectations

Other distractions we must be careful of are the use of alcohol, drugs, gangs, etc. The important thing to remember with these types of distractions is that if we instill a belief system in our children about these things, there is a better chance that they won't experiment with them. A great deterrent is to make them aware of the health issues involved with using alcohol, drugs, and cigarettes. There are free brochures available with very graphic photographs depicting the effects of alcohol, drug, and cigarette use. These brochures are readily available at many medical facilities, schools, and online. In addition, we must simply tell our children that the use of alcohol, drugs, and cigarettes is prohibited by law for them and that you will not tolerate them abusing their bodies and jeopardizing their futures.

These brochures are even a great way to encourage our children to abstain from pre-marital sex or at least protect themselves from disease and pregnancy by exposing them to the brochures that illustrate and discuss the very painful and grotesque diseases out there.

Keep their eyes on the prize

So, as parents we can also help our children stay focused by telling our children to keep it **R.E.A.L.**

Recognize disruptions

Eliminate or limit existing disruptions

Avoid inviting disruptions into their lives

Learn to picture themselves where they want to be in life

…And as parents we can help our children to stay focused by continuing to **C.A.R.E.**

Create the energy that fuels their dreams through activities / encouragement

Activities / Encouragement – Find events that showcase their career choices (If they want to be an actor/actress, take them to Broadway plays.)

Role models – Expose them to people that set good examples

Encouragement – Associate traits and characteristics they possess with those required in their chosen field of work

CHAPTER TEN

Unleashing Power

"Becoming who we were meant to be"

I believe that all of us have unique qualities that, when unleashed, become powerful tools and create an energy that ignites a passion to become who we were meant to be.

Each of us is powerful and talented in some way. There's possibility, potential, and greatness in all of us. We are all something special waiting to happen. Each of us is loved by our Creator and able to experience fresh beginnings. With every waking, there is opportunity. There is often little question of one's capability, but more of a question of one's ambition. Talent makes us capable, but discipline makes us great! Unleashing power is the way to greatness. So, what does it mean to unleash power?

Unleashing power is tapping into one's own internal resources. We do that by first helping our children recognize what is great about them. Sometimes what is great about our children may also be what they are most inspired by or love to do. Do they have a sense of humor, are they great listeners, do they sing like birds, are they great at math, reading, science, are they graceful and charismatic are they dramatic and suited for acting? Do they speak in a way that captures an audience, like a poet? Does your child write with the imagination of a great author? Once their greatness has been identified, we help them to own it by recognizing that this is something great about them. Have your child embrace what is great about them and teach them to nurture their greatness by practicing and enriching their knowledge in the subject. Help them to understand the intricacies of their greatness by researching all that they need to know to pursue a life supported by their passions. Expose them to others that serve as inspiration in their areas of interest.

As your child grows in their greatness, begin to help them set goals that will keep them focused and maturing into their greatness.

Tell your child that they can! Encourage them to keep dreaming because to dream and set goals is to have a vision, and every reality began with a vision.

God bless you and may God bless the dreams manifesting in your each of your children.

About the Author

In 1993 Les began a career as a Correctional Officer at one of the largest County Jails in the United States, which is where he discovered that many of the 10,000 detainees that were incarcerated had chosen very similar paths and had made similar choices, and that those choices had led them to jail. Armed with this information, Les began speaking to at risk kids and providing tours through the County Jail in an effort to redirect teens away from destructive paths. Les provided hope to thousands of kids who needed direction during hopeless times.

Over the next 2 decades, Les would become a voice of inspiration and hope that continues to empower many to dream again.

Les developed the parental guidance program "Shaping the Lives of our Children", which is currently available in more than 150 Public Schools at no cost to the schools. The program has been presented in public forums and continues to give parents that additional insight necessary to develop productive and driven individuals.

Les is the owner and founder of "ITC Consulting and Training, LLC", which provides corporate training, consulting, and professional development coaching.

He graduated from Chicago State University and is a state certified instructor in more than 20 subjects.

Les is currently a Detective, Crime Scene Investigator, and Juvenile Specialist with a County Sheriff's Police Department. As a state certified juvenile officer, Les has been able to offer troubled juveniles an optional path and direct them away from incarceration and criminal records.

Les is married and has four children, 3 of which are college students, a 13 year old, a son-in-law, and a grandson.

Les is a dynamic motivational speaker and is active in his community and in the church, where he continues to spread his belief that "Strong Families build Strong Communities!"

Printed in the United States
By Bookmasters